MW01596731

LAYOFF REBOOT:

BOUNCE BACK FROM JOB LOSS AND FIND A CAREER YOU LOVE

Courtney Kenney

Copyright © 2016 Courtney Kenney

CONTENTS

BONUS: Your *Layoff Reboot* workbook
This book is accompanied by a companion workbook that you can download for free from http://projectmanagerwriter.com/layoff-reboot.

With the workbook, you can follow along and capture:

1. Your **most important goals** in a simple chart.

2. A **daily schedule** that can guide how you spend your day if you, too, choose to reboot your career.

3. **Interest / Skills** – Not sure where to start? If you have many interests and can't decide where to focus, this may help.

1 SURPRISE! YOU'RE NO LONGER NEEDED

"You've been impacted."

Not the words I expected to hear from my boss one early spring morning. After fifteen years of hard work, the technology company I worked for in Chicago was struggling, and decided to let me go. I had become expendable. What was worse, my company was the only "home" I knew. I had landed a job with them immediately after college, and spent my entire career there.

My performance was solid, and I'd made significant contributions. Don't think a layoff can happen to you? Think again.

And then think again.

I didn't know it at the time, but losing my job was

the best thing for me. My layoff forced me to stop and think—deeply. Suddenly my world was upside down. My safety net and career identity were gone.

I knew I could go out and start job-hunting. As if sensing trouble, I'd been keeping my eye on the local job market for months already, and knew there were similar opportunities out there. But something held me back. Although surprised and disappointed, I also felt relief. I was off the hook from all the recent tedious aspects of work. Thoughts of a Chicago summer stretched out ahead of me. Was I supposed to feel this good about losing my job?

It took some time to admit, but I wasn't happy with what I was doing and hadn't been for some time. I didn't want to find a job just like my old one. I needed a change of environment. But even though I was ready to take a risk, I wasn't sure what to do next, or even where to start.

I gave myself three months to figure it out, and put aside my job search, embarking instead on a process to discover what I wanted to do next in my career. If I wasn't clear in my own head what job I wanted, how could I possibly talk to recruiters? But I'd worked such long hours, and dedicated so many years to my company, that I barely remembered what things I enjoyed, either.

Just as rebooting a computer system can fix an error, I wanted to "reboot" my career and life. I wanted to self-correct, and start over again.

Those three months, which I used to break from the 9-to-5 work life and experiment, turned into what I call my *layoff reboot*. In three months, I discovered what I love—writing—and immersed myself. I reconnected with the things that energize me and managed to go from words on paper to self-publishing my first book. I learned to love the process of turning my thoughts and ideas into a finished product.

Whether I make writing my full time career remains to be seen. But this would never have happened without my decision to "reboot." It wasn't just about taking a break; I threw myself entirely into this process. But learning more about myself—understanding what makes me tick—also means I'm more valuable to future employers. Now that I've woken my creativity, I realize anything is possible.

Have you recently lost your job, or do you think you're at risk of a layoff? Or maybe you're unhappy, and thinking of leaving on your own.

In this book, I'll walk you through my *layoff reboot* process. Using a variety of self-discovery tools, I realized my former job wasn't the right one for me. Now, when I'm ready to look for my next job, I have the knowledge to go after what energizes and excites me.

I wrote this to share my process. This book contains the tools I used and is for people who find themselves in an unexpected situation, whether it's a layoff, a sudden job loss, or resignation. What if you just need a nudge to try something new?

I hope sharing my story will make you see you aren't alone. Parts of my experience might be understood best by someone who's been through a layoff, but the process and tools I used can apply to many situations.

After reading this book, you'll be armed with techniques to 1) deal with your initial reaction to losing your job, 2) get organized, and 3) do your own *layoff reboot*—reinvent yourself by learning what you love to do and developing an action plan to make important life changes.

Why read this?

Getting laid off sucks. It's demoralizing. Many people think the company they work for is looking out for them, but in today's workplace there's no guarantee of long-term employment. In fact, today's workers are finding out they are more expendable than ever, as jobs are outsourced to an ever-changing list of "cheaper" locations.

According to outplacement firm Challenger, Gray & Christmas, job cuts in the technology sector rose 77 percent in 2014, with particularly high numbers of layoffs in the computer industry.

The solution to the disappointment of getting laid off is to use it to your advantage.

Losing your job is scary. But it's a rare opportunity to pause and reflect. What dreams have you been hanging on to? What will make you glad to get out of bed in the morning? By taking time to stop and restart my career—by rebooting—I finally found something that was meaningful to me.

I want to help you accomplish new things—things you thought were impossible. In the first month of my reboot, I wrote my first book (a dream since childhood) and established an action plan for the next two months that would allow me to pursue starting my own business. I also managed to fit in a two-week vacation and hours of industry training to keep me current.

I'll describe how I turned my layoff into a positive experience and ended up happier. Faced with job loss, I took time to reassess my interests, found what satisfies me, and what keeps me energized. I thought deeply about my goals in life and wrote them down. I then turned these into a workable plan. I'll show you how you can do the same.

What you end up doing next, though, is entirely up to you. Think of it as a "choose your own adventure" book. As a kid, I used to read a lot of these stories, always involving fantasy (think ogres, dwarves, and wizards). I remember the excitement of turning the pages. I felt so satisfied that I was making the choices about what the hero would do next. Even when, on the last page, she ended up locked in a dungeon or eaten by a dragon, I had created the adventure. Through the hero, I had taken a risk. And if I didn't like the ending, I could go back and choose something else.

My hope is this book will guide you not only back on your feet, but toward interests you've dreamed about pursuing for a long time. At the very least, you'll have learned a lot more about yourself. I myself discovered how I want to spend my time. I finally learned the answer to the question, "what do you want to be when you grow up?"

I hope you will too.

What to Expect

You'll need to put concentrated effort into making your reboot successful. You'll need to dedicate some time to reflecting, preparing, and creating your action plan. This time period can be as short or as long as you want. I spent a month making the mental shift and coming up with my plan. There's no magic "one-size-fits-all" to this. Everyone is different. You may be able to get everything done quicker, or you may need several months.

At the end of reading this book, you'll have an action plan tailored to YOU. You'll know next steps and be mentally prepared to start leading the life you want. Imagine the power of knowing what you want to do next. Whether it's a career change, becoming your own boss, or finding a new type of job in your field, you'll have an advantage over the competition. You'll have done the hard work of discovering what you love to do. Best of all, you'll have a plan.

Don't wait too long to start, though. I learned this the hard way, working unhappily for years only to get laid off. The longer you go without taking action and developing your plan, the harder it is to get back on track. Others may put pressure on you to find a job quickly. Resist.

Follow the steps I've laid out. You'll find a free companion workbook on my website projectmanagerwriter.com.

I wish you all the best in this next phase. Get prepared for an exciting journey. Congratulations, you get to decide what you want to do next!

2 LIFE BEFORE LAYOFF

Before I describe my layoff experience, let me share some background. I've had a tendency to be a workaholic and a perfectionist, and will throw myself into whatever I'm doing especially if I'm learning something new. This work ethic has a lot to do with my upbringing.

My grandfathers were both WWII vets and later took jobs for life with pensions. I had two tough, hardworking grandmothers.

My maternal grandmother grew up on a farm in Kansas and later joined the Navy as an officer, a significant accomplishment for a woman of her time. When she babysat, she was strict—no monkeying around. My other grandmother broke out her flyswatter whenever we kids acted up. Trust me, you didn't want to get wacked by that thing.

My parents instilled strong work ethics in me, as well. I grew up outside Washington, DC, where nearly every kid had parents in the government, including me. Their advice, like other baby boomer parents, was to work hard through school, find a good company job, and work from age 23 to 65. Save all you can along the way, and hopefully you'll have a good pension for your old age.

Following the advice they modeled, I worked hard at being a good student. I tested into the best available high school—a magnet program also attended, coincidentally, by Sergey Brin, Google cofounder. After the rigorous high school academics, I graduated from college with honors.

I had good success early in my career. My company was financially strong and I earned opportunities. In my first two years, I traveled to every major city in Canada on business. I volunteered for an expatriate assignment in Australia, and was accepted. There I met amazing people and traveled to exotic places. I did business in China and Singapore. I vacationed in New Zealand and New Caledonia.

Looking back, though, as much as I tried to appreciate my experience, my workaholic tendencies were already forming. I had anxiety about not being good enough, so I overcompensated. My U.S. coworkers told me I always seemed to be working. And I was. I was in the office by 9am, started conference calls at 5pm to catch European colleagues, and then ended with U.S. calls from 10pm until 2am. I kept up this fevered pace even when I returned to the States, but had a few good years within the corporate office. I got promoted, managed several great project teams, had fun, and traveled more.

But eventually, further up the corporate ladder, I wound up in a job that was wrong for my skillset. I learned this the hard way. I had a terrific, very successful project, but when it ended the job changed, and I became a number cruncher. Although I enjoyed analytics and could "compose symphonies in excel" (actual quote from a former boss), I didn't enjoy it enough to make it work long-term.

As good as I was at managing projects, the trouble was that once they ended, I didn't seem to enjoy managing what was left over. I was unhappy, and compensated the only way I knew how: by working insane hours. Four days of the week I was gone before my husband woke at 6am. I didn't get back until 8pm.

Finally I hit the breaking point, and told my boss I couldn't handle it anymore; that I wasn't happy. To my surprise, he was understanding and even helped me find my next job within the company doing what I was happiest with—managing projects.

In the next job, my new boss and I got along great, and together delivered a huge global project. Things went well for several years. Again, I moved to an operational role after the project ended. At the same time, I finally found a better work-life balance. I ditched the long commute after my office was relocated close to home. With the extra time I began regular workouts, took walks, and met friends after work.

My situation had improved, but I was still missing something. My working days were intense, and even before my layoff, my mind set had begun to change. I started reading books about entrepreneurship. A seed of an idea began to form. What if I could change the way I work, so I'm not constantly on call? What if I could work for myself and simplify what I do? What if all the hard work I'm putting in for my company could be refocused on myself?

Ultimately these thoughts were the basis of my reboot, and changed my perspective on work. But despite all my attempts to achieve balance, my workaholic tendencies made an appearance. These traits might never go away entirely. It's tough to undo years of hard wiring and being a "Type A" personality. Although it was only for three months, I got intensely wrapped up in my reboot process. But in the end, that was what it took to really reboot—to start over and self-correct.

Maybe it's less about trying to fight against my natural tendencies and go with the flow. Knowing that I'm a workaholic and a perfectionist, why should I work for someone else? Why not be a workaholic for myself? I learned I could create, produce, and live life on my own terms.

What drives you? How did your early life and family members shape your current career path?

3 WHY REBOOT?

My layoff seemed inevitable after years of company downsizing. When I started in 1999 I was one of more than 100,000 employees. As the years passed, the company's workforce shrank to a third its original size as pieces of the business were sold off and people were let go.

When my company eventually let me go too, my initial reaction ran from shock to dismay, even relief. At first, I could hardly comprehend it. And then the news started to sink in. Maybe this was inevitable. My company was cost cutting; this had happened to others before me. There had been talk of changes. I'd just had no idea how significant and sweeping they would be.

Some handled the news better than others, but the ones who bounced back fastest and most successfully had two things in common. First, they weren't bitter. They recognized that dwelling on the negative aspects of their situation was a bad use of energy. Second, they started taking action. I wanted to be part of that group.

I wanted to use my layoff as an opportunity to improve my life and become happier with my career.

The Problem

Those of us laid off had our lives disrupted, since many had worked at the company long-term, some upward of 20 years. But now that they'd been laid off, people were talking openly, and as I talked to people affected I noticed a common theme: people weren't happy with what they had been doing. And neither was I.

So why were we spending 40+ hours a week doing this?

I'd passed up a chance to take a voluntary severance package years before. I'd regretted that decision a number of times since. Back then, I wasn't sure how to go about making such a huge change. I was afraid to make the leap to try something else. I didn't know where to start.

I was afraid to quit even though I knew I was unhappy.

With my layoff, I was forced to make a change. I

quickly realized I didn't want to go back to the same type of job I had. I had gotten used to stress, politics, and dissatisfaction. I didn't want to deal with that anymore.

I began to articulate the ideas floating around in my head. Wouldn't it be great to finally write a book, or start a company and work for myself? Wouldn't it be nice if I could make my own rules and follow my own schedule? Once my layoff news finally sunk in, these thoughts rose up to the front of my mind again.

The Solution

Knowing I needed to act quickly—to seize a rare opportunity to take time off—I pulled together tools to see myself through the next few weeks. As a Project Manager, I knew the importance of getting a solid plan in place. And this time to reinvent myself and try my experiment was precious.

By reading this book, you'll learn how to get organized. I had to make a mindset shift from my employer (where my focus had long been) to myself. I'll show you how I brainstormed and created a roadmap of my goals. Lastly, I'll walk through how I created my action plan and used a daily schedule to keep myself on track.

With my tools, you can begin your own journey of self-discovery. Whether you're unemployed or not, learn how to identify and prioritize how you choose to spend your time—pursuing new interests that will help you find a career that truly interests you. With my tools, you'll start to accomplish more than you thought possible.

You may even change how you look at your life. It happened to me.

I took a rare opportunity to pause and attempt to reinvent myself. I gave myself a *layoff reboot*.

Making the Decision to Reboot

Taking time off isn't possible for everyone. Some of my former co-workers had to go job-hunting right away, out of necessity. There's nothing wrong with that, and it's possible to reinvent yourself even when fully employed. Some were happy with their chosen career or were breadwinners not ready to step away from a full-time job.

In my situation, I did the math to make things work. And we made sacrifices. I analyzed our budget and made efforts to save money by cooking more at home, and scrutinizing all purchases. A few temporary lifestyle changes would get us through the next three months.

My husband, and most of my friends, were supportive of what I had chosen to do. But not everyone got it. Some had a hard time wrapping their heads around the idea of reinvention. We've been programmed to accept more conventional jobs. You'll need to realize not everyone will understand what you're trying to do.

I know it's a tough concept for most people. In making my decision to stop and take a break, I asked myself, "What's the worst that could happen?" Even if I started job-hunting right away, it could take several months to find a job. After three months off, my worst case would be looking and not finding employment right away. If that happened, we'd have to dip into savings or drastically reduce expenditures. After discussing, my husband and I realized we could handle the worst case scenario. There would be a lifestyle change but one that was worth it if I could be ultimately happier.

If things worked out well—the best case scenario—I might find a new career direction. I would find something I was truly excited about. Knowing this meant I would find a way to make a new career choice work. Switching careers mid-way through life might mean less income, at least temporarily. There would need to be sacrifices, but I was okay with that. This was a chance to start over.

Even if my reboot failed, I would only be giving up three months of my life. In the grand scheme of things, that wasn't much. And ultimately, I decided this opportunity was too important to pass up. But then another concern popped up. How would a gap in my resume look if I decided to go back into the corporate world? My job loss was explainable—I was caught in a downsizing. I could build additional self-improvement activities into my reboot plan. I could take skill training and maybe volunteer somewhere. In future interviews, I would explain that although I wasn't job-hunting right away, I was working on adding new skills.

This break to pause and work on my reboot plan was life-changing. For me, there's nothing more important than how I spend my waking hours. I lacked energy and excitement in my old job. Now I was going to get that back.

Assuming you decide to take time and reboot, what's your best case scenario? What's the worst thing that could happen and how will you handle it?

4 YOU'RE OUT OF A JOB. NOW WHAT?

Getting told your job is being eliminated or you're no longer needed is hurtful. It doesn't matter whether you knew ahead of time. There's never a good time to receive this news.

Initially, I was surprised. These were some of the things that ran through my mind:

"I can't believe they let go of me."

"I knew there might be changes but I thought they'd wait a few more months."

"Don't they want me to finish project XYZ?"

"What about my team? What will happen to them?"

"Someone must have known. Why didn't

anyone tell me?"

"I can't believe _____ is staying over me!"

And on and on.

My emotions swung from disappointment to surprise to denial. The key is to realize that this is completely normal. We're human beings, and we're hard-wired to crave acceptance. But when you're in a layoff situation, it's best to take the high road. Yes, you have the right to feel anger and betrayal. Deal with these emotions as best you can. Talk to someone neutral. See a therapist if you need to.

Whatever you do, don't let your anger seep into the workplace environment you're leaving. It's not helpful for others getting laid off or for the people left to carry on afterwards, who had no say in layoff decisions.

And keep in mind that it's a small world. You never know who will end up making a hiring decision about you someday. The classier you make your exit, the likelier you'll be remembered as someone who was respectful and good to have around.

48 Hour Cooling Off

I decided to tell my two employees about my news right away. I wanted them to hear about it from me.

Beyond them, I told only my husband immediately.

I wanted to have a 48 hour "cooling off" period before I started telling family, friends, and coworkers.

If you're faced with job loss, I recommend you give yourself a day or two to work through your initial reaction too. I needed time to process. I didn't want to lose my cool when telling people. What would others think? What would my family say?!

The day I found out, I went home and spent the evening discussing things with my husband. He completely supported my idea to avoid telling people right away. We took a long walk. Luckily it was a nice summer's day, and we headed to our favorite local pub with a notebook to start writing things down.

Get Your Thoughts on Paper

When you get the news, you'll have a million thoughts swirling through your head. Once you break the news to your significant other and closest family and friends, you'll have even more ideas and external input.

To make things easier, try writing down a list of things on your mind. What's worrying you? Are there practical things you want to be sure you address? Get them down on paper.

Here's what I wrote down the first two days after getting notified:

Things to do right away

1. Figure out how to tell my family and closest friends

2. Update resume

3. Update LinkedIn profile

4. Get in touch with people on LinkedIn

Things to do this weekend

1. Figure out next steps for benefits such as medical, dental, life insurance

2. Read through my exit material

3. Determine if I need to get any doctor appointments scheduled

Things to do before my last day

1. Make sure I give my personal contact information to people (phone, email)

2. Update my contact list and get in one place

3. Complete work hand-off

What I will change NOW

1. Connect with at least one new person or acquaintance every day

2. Exercise daily (For me this meant starting a free online 30-day yoga challenge. I needed something physical to stay sane.)

3. Start a practice of writing daily and journaling

Doing this initial short list will help you get some of your immediate thoughts on paper and out of your head. This was important for me and cut down on my immediate stress.

That first week, I ended up feeling physically fatigued due to the emotional highs and lows. I craved junk food. I didn't have much energy and I got a cold. Maybe my body was giving up its last remnants of stress attached to my former job.

Telling People the News

Be prepared to feel some shame when you tell family and friends what's happened. This surprised me. I was a good worker. I knew this. But I still felt I'd been singled out somehow, even though I wasn't the only one laid off.

It's good to try to frame the news positively. This will probably be hard, and won't come naturally.

You can try something like what I told people: "I was laid off. So were some of my co-workers. I have mixed emotions—I'll miss my colleagues but I'm looking forward to new opportunities ahead. It's an exciting time." This explanation addressed what happened—the fact I was caught up in a layoff—without dwelling on why. This also showed I was feeling disappointed but choosing to focus on the opportunities ahead of me.

You shouldn't need to say much beyond this. If people press, you can simply say, "I'm taking time off to think, and come up with a plan for what I want to do next."

When I said this, everyone got it. Who doesn't want summer off?

Some people tried to be helpful and sent jobs my way, and I made sure to follow up on any outreach and continued to expand my network. I talked to recruiters about jobs several times. I even had an interview. But then I had to remind myself what path I was on. Rushing back into the job hunt wasn't for me. I owed it to myself to take a break and focus on fine-tuning my goals. I had confidence I would end up happier in the long run. I politely told recruiters I would be available in another three months, that until then, I was taking personal time off.

The world didn't end. They understood.

5 GET ORGANIZED

After losing my job, I spent a few weeks thinking, talking with close friends, and keeping busy with social events. I reached out to other colleagues I knew were impacted. I set up lunches and happy hours. I wanted to discuss what we were going through, and figured there was safety in numbers. It's important to connect with others especially in the early stages, and I'm glad I took time to do this, to heal a bit.

Most importantly, I gathered the courage to start telling more people in my circle of friends. I didn't come out with it right away. If someone asked me how work was going, I would tell them. If I found a pause in conversation where it made sense, I told friends one-on-one. I didn't want the news to put a damper on things. After all, this was a positive experience for me.

It made it easier that many of my friends had been in the same situation at some point in their career. A layoff wasn't the badge of shame I was expecting especially since the 2008 financial crisis, when it became quite common.

More surprisingly, as I talked to more people laid off from my company, I found out that they also wanted to take a break. I'm not sure why this was such a surprise to me. Maybe I thought I was the only one going through this "crisis." But I felt relieved. If so many of my friends were going through this, there must be a lot of people out there who wanted the same thing.

Pulling away from work and saying farewell

One of the most awkward things about my transition was my hand-off period, when some of my coworkers pulled away and stopped including me in meetings and projects. The funny thing was, I'd seen this before. I myself had been guilty of not contacting people once I knew of their impending layoff. Back then, I had worried about bothering them and wanted to give them space.

But it hurt now that it was happening to me. If they could drop me that quickly, was I valued? Was my work even significant?

The answer is yes. I knew I had been valued. Close colleagues told me repeatedly how much I'd be missed. But people want to avoid discomfort.

Continuing to contact me or include me in meetings meant they would then feel obligated to say something. This wasn't about me personally. They just wanted to avoid a difficult situation.

Two colleagues in particular were the exception and were wonderful during my transition. Both continued to work with me even when uncomfortable. They spent time with me when I asked for it and remained supportive.

But even if you don't have people like this at your work, stay strong. You can get through this. While you spent a lot of time with your colleagues, get ready to start moving on and start focusing on a new plan for yourself.

Now You Are #1

If there's anything I want you to learn from this book and realize early, it's this: <u>you are your number one priority going forward</u>.

I repeat: you are your first priority. This is a critical shift in thinking. You don't owe your company anything beyond completing your transition and keeping their information confidential.

My *layoff reboot* only really began once I understood I was in charge of finding my own path forward. I wanted to find meaningful work. To achieve this, I had to purposefully decide how to spend the coming weeks. At the end of my journey,

I wanted to look back on this experience as one where I made huge strides without regrets.

If you have a transition period, do what you can to hand off your work right away. You'll have plenty of other things to fill time. I was surprised how quickly my days filled up.

Don't prolong the transition period or try to hang on to work. If you're hanging on to some shred of hope that they'll change their minds and ask you to stay, realize this is unlikely.

And start declining meetings as soon as you can. Most importantly, make it clear to your coworkers you're not accepting new work during this phase.

I was able to use the time between layoff notification and my last day to process the news, hand off work and get most of my finances and benefits sorted. But avoid the temptation to check out entirely. Stay available to your colleagues and offer help if they need it. I was still providing them information even during my final days at the company. It's simply good karma.

Make Lists

Once you've handled any remaining work priorities, I recommend making several lists to start getting organized. The goal is to get you ready to move on to something new as you prepare to work full time to discover what you love and ultimately get on the path to a more fulfilling career.

List 1: Benefits/Financial

First, list out any financial transition items you need to take care of. This should be anything work-related impacted by your leaving. For example, mine contained bank accounts I would need to change and how to continue my medical/dental benefits and life insurance.

I recommend making this within a few days of being notified. Consider it a form of therapy as these items impact you and your family's well-being and security. Taking care of them right away will help ease your mind.

To organize, you can create a spreadsheet with tabs for each category.

1. Payments to expect (e.g., vacation time payout)

2. Retirement savings such as 401(k)

3. Health benefits

4. Bank accounts

Keep track of all notes on phone calls you make regarding benefits. This keeps your information in one place for easy reference down the road. Also include necessary tasks such as handing in your work computer, shredding files, migrating your contact list, and setting up a new personal calendar or email accounts.

This exercise helps you "clean house" and opens up much-needed mental space. Once complete, you will be a step further to closing the chapter on one job to start focusing on the future.

List 2: Interests / For Fun

The next list is a lot more fun. Start listing things that interest you but that you've been putting off because you were too busy. What ideas have been rattling around up there inside your head?

I had fun with my list which you can see below. I included anything that popped into my head no matter how silly or far-fetched. There were things I had dreamed about for a long time, or that I'd talked about but never had time for. Things I'd been putting off. My list also included habits and lifestyle changes I wanted to make.

I knew not all these things would happen, but the idea was to have fun and dream.

-Write and publish a book

-Develop the habit of writing every day

-Lose weight / get toned

-Learn to cook a few amazing, easy meals that will impress friends and family

-Learn Wordpress to start blogging

-Learn how to sew sock monkeys

-Volunteer regularly with a local charity

-Read daily

-Visit Paris and Italy

-Laugh more

-Go to museums and attend art lectures

-Go on a meditation retreat

-Become sought after as an expert in a certain field

-Travel to the Pacific Northwest

-Travel to Japan

-Learn how to podcast

-Swim with whale sharks

-Learn sword fencing

-Write and direct a movie

-Start a publishing firm

-Attend Comic-Con

-Start painting art (great stress relief)

-Get a massage

-Learn about minimalism. Reduce clutter in your house.

Get the idea? I loved doing this, and could have listed more. This process made me realize all the things I could do when I didn't have the demands of a full-time job holding me back.

I kept a notebook with me to jot down ideas as they came up, and added to my list over time. I still keep it in case I'm struck with new ideas. The list also helps keep me on track as I grow and develop. Things that interested me ten years ago were much different than what interests me today.

I refer to this list monthly as a sanity check, because I don't ever want to be in a position again where I'm not checking things off this list. From now on, I want to always be tackling my "fun list."

List 3: Networking Contacts

I also made a list of people to connect with. It was helpful to list out former coworkers, past mentors and friends I hadn't been in contact with recently.

As I made this list, I gradually started contacting a few people through email, LinkedIn, and Facebook to let them know my situation. When I reached out,

I explained I'd been laid off. I wanted to hear how they were doing and to wish them well. I also let them know I was taking time off for a much needed break. This was important, but not because I needed anything from them.

A huge lesson I learned was how much I had let my network deteriorate over the last few years. I suspect this happens a lot nowadays with the constant information flow and less individual face time. I wanted to rekindle relationships, because my priorities had gone way off course. Since shifting my focus back to me, I realized I was the one to blame for not keeping in touch. I let anxiety and fear of changing my job keep me immobilized. I spent more time worrying about my job performance and less on maintaining relationships.

My hope is you've done a great job in keeping up with your friends and social network. For me, I needed to reconnect, and this was an important step for me following my layoff.

List 4: Housekeeping

This is where you list any administrative tasks you need to take care of. It may not be much fun, but nevertheless these are things that need to get done.

My own list included home projects like painting and repairs, cleaning up old files, and organizing closets and cabinets. I also included trip planning. My husband and I had planned a late summer vacation, and I added items such as booking flights, lodging and scheduling.

Establish a Morning Routine

This was a game changer for me. Once my job ended, I felt a bit lost. I spent two weeks feeling sorry for myself and wondering what to do. I cleaned up some of the clutter in my house, but nothing was moving me forward mentally.

And then something clicked. I realized I needed to seize this opportunity to work on important goals. I didn't want to come away in one or two months wondering what had happened to all the time I had. I was already noticing how fast time was flying since I'd been notified.

To get out of this rut, I established a morning routine. My mission was to stick with it. First, I thought about how much time I had available each morning. You'll need to assess your own obligations, such as seeing kids off to school, and work these into your morning.

For me, I knew writing was my number one goal. So I allocated one hour of my morning—every morning—to writing. I also needed to work out consistently, even if I could only squeeze in 10-15 minutes. I wanted to do something to get my body active. Finally, I had always wanted to develop a daily habit of meditation.

When you think about what you want to accomplish in your morning routine, think of two or three important habits you want to develop. Maybe you're a programmer, and you want to develop the habit of coding at least two hours each day. The key to developing habits is finding the discipline to tackle these things consistently.

When I worked full-time, I wanted to write daily but found it difficult to muster up energy after a full day or work, commuting, family time, etc. Think of your brain as a gas tank. All the minutia, daily decisions, and interactions with people deducts mental space from a full tank.

If possible, avoid computer or phone screen time until you complete your morning routine. Once you start doing emails or checking your twitter feed, you're depleting your mental energy.

Imagine if you could knock out your most important goal FIRST thing. Since I started adhering to my daily routine, my productivity has tripled. I feel a genuine sense of accomplishment.

My morning routine looked something like this:

> **7:30-8:00** – Get up, grab coffee and journal for 5 minutes about things I'm grateful for. This gets me into a positive mindset for the rest of my day.

8:00-9:00 – Writing. I set a timer and wrote for one hour (I started off at 30 minutes first, then 45, eventually working my way up to a full hour).

9:00-9:30 – Meditate for 5 minutes, followed by exercise—either 15 minutes of yoga (I used free online 30-day challenge videos at home) or 20 minutes of intense, rest-based exercise (think squats and free weights, also at home).

During my writing time, I'll generally work on a project, such as book or a blog, but if I'm not feeling inspired to write, I make lists of ideas. For example, I'll write down 10-15 ideas such as "Ideas to Procrastinate Less" or "Ideas to have more fun."

If something is bothering or worrying me, making a list of ideas is a great way to get my brain going. The particular topics aren't necessarily important; what works is you're practicing that habit, sticking to your routine, and developing the discipline to get your most important goal accomplished early each day.

If exercise is part of your morning routine, you have to find out what works for you through trial and error. I'm a big believer in high-intensity, short-duration workouts, and they can be done at home. Years ago, I thought you had to go to the gym or do cardio for long periods to stay fit, and with my busy work life, I didn't have time or energy to go even a few times a week.

I learned about shorter workouts from reading a book called *PACE: The 12-Minute Fitness Revolution*. It's a fast read, and the author includes case studies and shows before and after photos. I also found a company called MetabolicEffect.com which has articles and free weekly workout videos.

Part of my process was spending five minutes journaling to debrief on how my morning routine was progressing. I've found this helpful in determining where to make tweaks. For example, I originally did meditation and workouts first before writing. But I was procrastinating, because I didn't always want to start working out right away. This ended up delaying my writing time (ultimately more important to me). So I switched to writing first thing. This helped me get back on track. Journaling about my experience helped me become more self-aware of what was working and where I needed to self-correct.

If you later get bored with your routine, try switching things up.

Bottom line, have fun with figuring out what works for you! Nailing your routine is a critical step in really immersing yourself in your rediscovery. Through discipline each morning, I wrote 700-1,000 words daily (eventually getting me to my goal of publishing my first book).

Try your new routine for at least two weeks. You'll start to notice improvements AND get a lot accomplished.

Mental Purging

After my layoff, I often felt overwhelmed. I was used to being on top of things when I worked as a Project Manager, so this was unsettling. So far, I had made lists and established a morning routine, but I didn't know how to start moving forward. I wasn't sure how to go about discovering what I wanted to do next.

So I thought about why this was. There was a lot on my mind and I felt unsettled. I knew from past experience that when I have "mental clutter"—things weighing on my mind—I'm less effective. And that's when I realized I needed to do some "mental purging" before I could start working on my *layoff reboot*. Here's what I did working a few hours over a three-day span:

Day 1

A) Email clutter - I was hanging on to many articles I would get to "someday." They were taking up mental space. So I deleted them. I also unsubscribed to most newsletters, keeping them only if I thought they'd add value to the things on my interest list. I could always go seek something out if, after deleting, I decided I needed it again.

B) Computer desktop - Every time I turned on my computer, I saw too many icons. I worked on getting rid of things I wouldn't need. I wanted to have an uncluttered space to start fresh, since I would be using my computer to create and organize my activities.

C) Work space - I designated a clean work space. I valued having a single spot where I worked on my new plan. This needed to be uncluttered so I could have the mental energy to be creative.

Day 2

A) Papers and old files - I happen to be a "pile" person. When busy, I'll let things accumulate into piles instead of taking care of them right away. I spent an hour shredding old, irrelevant work papers from years past.

I'm a fan of the book, *Getting Things Done: The Art of Stress-Free Productivity* by David Allen. A key principle is to get things out of your head and onto a list that you work through methodically. But I took this one step further, and made sure all my things had a "home." As new things came in that I needed to deal with (emails, texts, mail) they went on a calendar, got filed, or added to my to-do list.

For example, if I got invited to have lunch with a friend, I set up the appointment immediately in my calendar. This way I took care of it right away *and* would have a reminder later.

B) Evernote - I used Evernote to store notes, ideas, and articles. I like the tool because it's available across devices—phone, computer, and tablet. I archived old and irrelevant notes, and spent a few minutes cleaning out old folders. Evernote is searchable, so I would have access should I need something in the future.

Day 3

A) Computer folders - This was my biggest challenge. Over the last two years I'd let some of my computer files get disorganized. I hadn't looked at my folder structure in a long time. I knew this would be the biggest clean up to tackle, so I blocked four hours.

Consider any mental clutter you might be hanging onto. How can you clear some space to focus on yourself?

6 PREPARE TO REBOOT

Now it's time to address priorities. Remember that Benefits/Financial list? First things first. Be sure to tackle anything on this list that needs handling.

Without a job, you'll want to be sure your benefits are sufficient to ensure no gap in coverage.

Then take some time to review your budget. Review recent credit card and bank statements, and list where you're spending money. Are all items essential? Can you live without some things for a few months? Can you consolidate certain expenses such as cable, phone, and internet?

An idea that worked for me was designating one day a month as "shopping day." My husband got on board as well. We could only buy items (we generally shop online) on one designated day per month. We chose one Saturday out of the month and this helped us stop impulse shopping. Throughout the month, I kept a wish-list that I saved until shopping day. By the time I could buy, I couldn't always recall why I'd thought I needed some of the items.

Physical space – Create your work zone

A good physical space in which to work is important. Designate a space that fosters creativity. Ideally this should be somewhere private and free of interruptions.

You'll need basic tools to stay connected and create your new plan. Are your tools—computer, phone, etc.—all sufficient?

Make sure your work environment is clean. Spend time decluttering if you need to. You'll want to have enough space available to work on your computer and also to write/draw/create when necessary.

After I cleared out old work files, papers, and folders, I tossed or donated knick-knacks. If I couldn't decide, I stored the item in a box for my cellar. I could rotate items every six months. The less physical stuff in your work zone, the more mental space you'll have to create.

Try to maintain a workspace separate from where you spend the rest of your time. This can be difficult when you live in a small place. I kept my things in a designated spot for when I started my morning routine so that, ideally, I could pick up every day where I left off—and when my day ended, I could pull away and disconnect, allowing me to focus on family time, leisure, etc.

If you're tight on space, it's a good idea to try to set up some kind of physical barrier such as a curtain or a folding screen to separate your work area. At a minimum, designate a drawer where you put away your things and can easily access them when you start your day.

Health

Your physical and mental well-being is going to take a beating after a layoff, so it's critical to keep your body and spirits up.

Getting adequate sleep is important. I recommend using a Fitbit or other wearable device to track your sleeping habits. Aiming for a full eight hours, I find going to bed and getting up on a regular schedule helps me meet my body's sleep needs. And if you're having a lot of trouble sleeping, see your doctor. For me, sleep was critical to have the energy to get up each morning and work on my action plan.

Wearable devices or smart phones can be used to track daily walking activity which should be between 8,000-10,000 steps per day. I was amazed to find how little walking I was doing when I first started using my Fitbit.

Walking, especially outside in nature, is fantastic for stress relief. Walk in a forest or park if you can. It lets your brain switch gears, and can jump-start your creativity.

If you go to the gym or do fitness classes, keep it up. If not, consider joining a gym or finding an online "30-day challenge"—there's tons of them out there. I started with a yoga challenge which only took 15-20 minutes per day. Friends of mine do various body part "challenges" such as abs, legs and arms. Exercise is important for stress relief, and the endorphins released can make you feel better.

Equally important as sleep and fitness is nutrition. Food is your fuel for your brain and creativity. I chose to eat a diet of mainly protein and vegetables, while limiting carbs, but choose what's right for you.

Productivity tools

Before we get into the next section, you'll want to set up productivity tools. Taking a few days to do this helped me get the most out of my time off.

This process includes establishing a reliable calendar system. With my work calendar gone, I moved everything to Google calendar. Now I can share calendars with my husband, and we keep a social calendar of the events and travel plans we've committed to. We always check this before anything gets scheduled.

Second, determine what system you'll use for storing information. During your *layoff reboot*, you'll be creating and learning at a fast pace. You'll want to have a way to store your notes and organize yourself.

The simplest solution is to create a set of folders on your computer. You can organize folders by topic. For example, my folders were: 1) Career/Jobs, 2) Writing, 3) Volunteering. I added to this later as new interests popped up.

Or you can also use Evernote, which I used to store notes and other information. They even have add-ons you can use to send online articles to an Evernote folder for later reading. And these files are searchable, so it's easy to find things once you've saved them.

Other ideas for getting organized:

1. Create a master Excel spreadsheet with multiple tabs for each topic area (e.g., writing, programming, etc.). Use this to store all your notes, learnings, tasks in one spot.

2. Set up a master Word document and create topic headings. Using the navigation pane, you can see topics at a glance and add to each section as needed.

3. Use paper folders to organize by topic and store in a filing cabinet.

The key is to find a solution that works for you. Everyone's different, and there's no one-size-fits-all solution. What you choose will depend on a number of factors—including how often you tend to get distracted.

Social media gets me sidetracked. I can easily spend too much time on Facebook, Twitter, and news sites. So I try not to visit these sites until afternoon, when I've completed my morning routine. I also challenge myself to cut down the time I spend on them. I use Rescuetime, a free tool you can install on your computer to track productivity. The tool measures your computer activity and emails you a weekly report with a productivity score.

Using Rescuetime, I can see how much time I'm spending on social media versus creating content in Word or Excel. During the writing of this section, my weekly report showed I spent 50 hours, 34 minutes on my computer (more than the previous week), but my productivity score was 72%, up from the previous week. I'm a statistics junkie, and this told me I'm getting better at cutting down on social media.

The nice thing about Rescuetime is you can customize the rankings of productive versus non-productive time in a way that's relevant for you.

Summary

Once you've spent some time to prepare, you'll have

cleared more mental energy to focus on your *layoff reboot*. Try your best to set up your physical space, productivity tools, and achieve a good health balance before you get started on the next phase. But remember to be patient with yourself.

Nobody's perfect, and the point of working on these things is to make your overall experience easier and more rewarding. I'm still working on these things myself. I went through spurts at times where I didn't work out or ate bad food. Having bad days here and there is part of the process, but it's fine as long as you're able to start over the next day.

If you're short on time, I recommend you focus on just a few critical things. To me, the most important things are: 1) getting eight hours of sleep, 2) eating more protein and vegetables, and 3) walking at least 30-60 minutes each day.

If nothing else, these things can really help you feel good enough to move your focus to the next phase.

7 DISCOVER WHAT YOU LOVE

Now comes the best part—discovering what you want to do next. This is the part where you reflect on your hobbies and interests. Here, you'll learn how I narrowed in on a single, big goal, and how you can do it too. Once you know what it is you can begin a plan that will fully engage you.

If you've read this far, you're making great progress. Like me, you're ready for something new. Perhaps your skills weren't a good fit for what you were doing. Maybe you loved your industry when you first started, but in recent years it's grown stale.

Perhaps, like I was, you are living each day going through the motions, trying to make it through another week. My identity had been wrapped up in my career—in my series of jobs with one company— that I nearly forgot who I was outside of it.

It's time to seize the moment and find out what truly energizes you. And once you find out what you love, you're one of the lucky few.

As you've been reading and doing pre-work, you've probably been thinking about what might come next. Maybe you already have ideas in your head. Hopefully you've captured those thoughts on your **Interests/For Fun List**. If not, don't worry. I'll walk you through how to capture your interests and get those thoughts down on paper.

This is an exciting time. For me, I needed to take care of all the upfront stuff first —getting a morning routine in place, clearing my physical space, and starting a regular workout and healthy eating habits. It took a few days for me to get used to having a new routine, but the payoff was good. For the first time in years, I was dedicating time to focus on me.

When was the last time you spent time working on self-improvement? Perhaps you've focused on work or other pressures for a long time. It can be incredibly freeing to focus on yourself for a time. This can be your time to develop long-neglected interests.

Here are the steps I followed during my *layoff reboot*.

Step One: Create a Mind Map

The first step I took was brainstorming about my goals. An easy way of doing this is by using a mind map. I originally called it "My Summer Break." But I wanted this to be more than just taking time off from work. I wanted this to be a real change, and I wanted to accomplish something great. So I changed it to "My Entrepreneur Experiment"-- three months to throw myself into a big goal, and see whether I was successful.

Have you encountered the technique of mind mapping before? Elementary schools sometimes use it to help kids plan essays. But even as an adult, it's the best tool I've found for releasing creativity and coaxing your brain into pumping out ideas. I had success with the approach when planning large projects. I also used a mind map to plan out writing this book. It's a tool I go back to again and again because it works so well.

The first thing you do is write down a central theme or idea. Next, you write down related ideas, so they form branches off your central theme. Get these on paper in any order they come into your head. No editing—the idea is to get all your thoughts down and let your creativity flow. As you keep writing down ideas, you'll even develop sub-branches. This keeps you brainstorming and captures all your thoughts on one page.

The point of this is to map out your major goals and

interests as you embark on your *layoff reboot*. Do you want to start a business? Brainstorm all related ideas that you have around that topic. If you already have business ideas, list those out and then start to detail additional thoughts.

For example, if your business idea is to provide software consulting services, what does that mean? What services do you provide? List those as separate bubbles, e.g., mobile app development, website development, etc. How will you deliver those services? Facebook apps, iTunes, or some other avenue entirely? Are there things you need to learn first? Do you need to brush up on marketing?

Get creative with your central theme. Here are some ideas:

-My Career Change Goals
-Starting My Own Business
-My Next Adventure
-Working for Myself
-How I'll Change the World
-My Mini-Retirement

I recommend using a large sheet of paper and starting in pencil. Some people like adding color and pictures. Do whatever works best for you. This should be a fun process—after all, you're idea mapping about yourself! What more interesting topic is there?

Hang onto the map when you're finished, and refer

back to it as you work through more exercises. It's meant to be a foundational tool, and my own mind map went through several iterations. I recommend you keep it in pencil at first and later go back with pen/color.

Have fun. Add wacky stuff. Play music while you're dreaming up new ideas.

You'll want to refer to your **Interests/For Fun list**. Consider those items as you create your mind map. For general items such as "read more books," include it on your mind map and then try to add specifics. For example, adding "read a new science fiction book a month" gives more concrete information that can later be turned into an action plan.

Aim for a few hours to focus on your mind map without distraction. Think of it as the foundation to determining how you'll spend your time over the next few months. This is a key input into your action plan.

There may be things you want to include but aren't sure about. Add them anyway with a question mark. For example, I wanted to learn about meditation and mindfulness. I considered going to a mindfulness retreat, but wasn't sure if my budget and schedule would allow. I included this thought, figuring I can remove it later if I decided against it.

When your mind map is done, take a break. Get a

good night's sleep so your thoughts can solidify before you start step two.

Step Two: Prioritize and Focus on One BIG Goal

With a fresh brain the next morning, I prioritized what I had mapped. I started by giving my mind map a sanity check. Were the ideas actually things I wanted to spend time on? After all, I would spend the next three months engaged in these activities—a huge change after fifteen years in a traditional 9-to-5 job.

I then considered the point of view of a stranger. Would my mind map be easy for someone else to grasp? Were themes grouped in such a way to be understandable? Was there enough specificity about what I'm trying to accomplish?

Ask yourself these questions and then spend a few minutes tweaking your map. But don't try for perfection. Avoid "analysis paralysis." The point is to get to "done" and move on. I ended up making tweaks several times over the next week, but the main structure never went away; I just added details and ideas as they came up.

If you're stuck for ideas and aren't sure what your direction is, don't worry. You're not alone. When I started this process I wasn't sure either. All I knew was I didn't want to go back to the 9-to-5 until I'd figured out my alternatives.

Creating a Venn diagram helped me get perspective. My three circles were: 1) My experience, 2) Dream Career, and 3) Back-up Career.

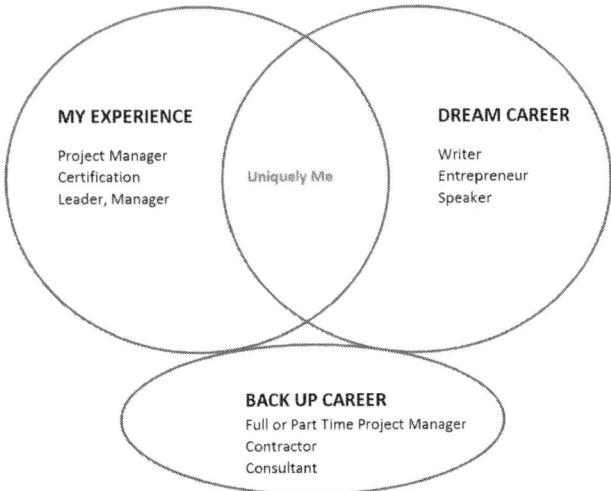

MY EXPERIENCE

Project Manager
Certification
Leader, Manager

Uniquely Me

DREAM CAREER

Writer
Entrepreneur
Speaker

BACK UP CAREER
Full or Part Time Project Manager
Contractor
Consultant

This helped me envision my unique combination of experience and credentials as a Project Manager, my dream job as a Writer/Entrepreneur, and a back-up plan just in case. For me, this meant I could go back and look for a full time job or contract as a Project Manager—but only after I'd given myself those three months to take a shot as an entrepreneur.

Having a backup plan in place is the Project Manager in me. Managing risk and contingency planning is a huge part of my background. For fifteen years, my job was to look for what might go wrong and get a plan in place to either avoid problems, or deal with issues as they happen. Of course, part of this was also inspired by fear of the unknown. I didn't think I had a single passion or "calling" in life for a long time. I thought something was wrong with me.

But after I undertook this process of self-discovery, I was able to pinpoint my unique skills and talents and realize I *do* have a calling. I uncovered the interests that fuel me. Had I not set aside time following my layoff, I would have missed out.

Maybe you don't have a single calling yet. But I bet you have skills that, when combined with your greatest interests, will give you a clear sense of purpose and is uniquely "you." For me, there was something important missing from my old job. I was using my expertise in project management, but I had lost an essential ingredient—creativity. In the end, this was the reason I was unhappy. The people I've met who are happiest with their careers are those who discovered what really drives them—what energizes them.

Try this Venn diagram exercise for yourself. Do you have two or three strong interests? Write them down. How can you combine them in a unique and interesting way? Is there a piece missing?

When I began, I knew virtually nothing about starting my own business from scratch. I knew I would need time over the next three months, during my experiment, to learn as much as I could about being an entrepreneur.

The last branches of my mind map included concrete things I wanted to accomplish. This ranged from big goals (e.g., "publish a book") to developing habits (e.g., "read more every day.").

Although I had many interests and ideas, the winning combination for me was combining writing and entrepreneurship with project management. With fifteen years invested in project management and a professional certification, I had a lot of existing knowledge to draw upon. But I knew I would need to learn new skills to turn a passion for writing into something marketable. My own success would come from combining these skills in non-traditional ways to generate income. I drew a triangle to keep these primary areas of focus top of mind:

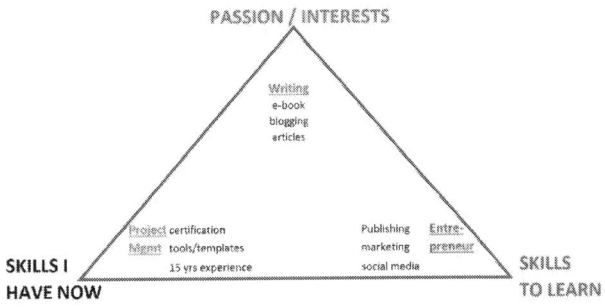

The key passion or interest I want to pursue—writing—was at the top. Bottom left was my existing skillset—Project Management. Completing the triangle were the "skills I want to learn"—working for myself. I added a few details within each area to give specifics.

Many people haven't thought to this level or done this sort of self-examination. But by mind mapping and exploring new directions, you'll be ahead of the game simply by having a plan and goals to reach for. Imagine being able to pursue what you truly want to do by combining your existing skills and new skills that you'll acquire!

Ranking Questions

Which elements of the mind map are most important to you? Figuring that out may take an hour or so of focused time. The purpose is to narrow your focus. My finished mind map had ten main branches, seven sub-branches and 38 separate items I wanted to accomplish. Whew. That would have been overwhelming!

There's no way I could achieve all that in three months. Time to whittle down to a few most important items.

The point is to be realistic about what you'll actually get done. You'll be raring to go once you start this journey, but unexpected demands on your time will inevitably crop up.

Confucius said a "person who chases two rabbits catches neither." I can't take on too many new things at once either. Consider your own capacity for change. If your focus is too broad, you may end up frazzled and burned out, and that's just discouraging and stressful.

It pays to be selective in how you spend your time

during your l*ayoff reboot.* I was tempted to add a lot to my plate. For example, I would have loved to travel, attend museum lectures, or attend that mindfulness retreat, but I knew I wouldn't be successful without a clear focus.

I recommend putting your less important mind map goals on the backburner for later.

To help me narrow my focus, I spent several minutes answering a few questions:

1. Which one thing on my mind map will I be most proud to accomplish?

Answer: Writing and publishing my first book.

2. Which is the second thing I would be most proud to finish?

Answer: Starting a blog and website for my new business.

3. Which items are habits (i.e., could become part of my routine)?

Answer: I had a ton! The most important ones were:

-Write daily

-List 10 new business ideas per day

-Do yoga daily

-Meditate daily

4. Which items are goals that will help me achieve my top two proudest accomplishments? Specifically, what outcomes should I expect?

Answer: My most important goals were to:

-Have my first published book.

-Obtain 20-30 continuing project management credits.

-Increase LinkedIn connections by 50%.

-Read five books about entrepreneurship.

-Set up my first website.

5. Which items are specific, time-bound events (e.g., can be scheduled in my calendar)?

Answer: Weekly meditation class, and social events with friends.

6. Which items are non-negotiable and must get done?

Answer: Schedule family vacation, and daily writing so I could finish a book.

These questions helped narrow my focus. I knew

my most important goal was writing, and if nothing else, I wanted to come out of this three-month experiment with a completed book in hand.

What takeaway from your mind map can you best visualize? For me, it was being able to tell people I wrote a book. I imagined myself asked to explain my job gap in an interview someday. I would be able to say I took time off to publish a book. Best of all, I would have the proof to show them.

By narrowing your focus, you should end up with your top two most important mind map items. These are the goals you'll want to focus on completing. If you end up with only one goal, that's fine. I use two in my examples since that's where I chose to focus.

I struggled with the temptation to add a third or even fourth goal, though. But it was time to be honest with myself. I didn't want to get overwhelmed, and I knew that could happen very easily. **I made a conscious decision to focus on only one big goal during my _layoff reboot_.**

Time management

After my layoff, I found myself facing a huge time management challenge. When I worked full time, my day organized itself. I lived by my outlook calendar, which was packed with back to back meetings or tasks. With this structure gone, I felt adrift, but I knew the key to being successful with this time off was discipline.

Other people I knew who successfully navigated layoffs set their alarm clock each morning and had a structured routine. They planned their days ahead of time.

Knowing my own tendencies, too much unstructured time would leave me struggling. For this reason, I needed a clear vision of my goals. I needed to put routines in place.

A pie chart helped me structure my days. I used it as a tool to make sure I focused on truly important items.

Instructions:

1. Draw a circle on a piece of paper.

2. Draw a line down the middle. Add another line from the halfway mark so you have one side split into two quarters.

3. Write your most important mind map goal on the 50% side. This is the biggest thing you want to accomplish and it's a must-do.

4. Next, write your second most important goal in one of the quarter sections. In the last quarter section, write "Family, Health, and Miscellaneous."

And then step back. Do your two goals reflect how you want to spend most of your time? Will you be happy at the end of your *layoff reboot*?

In my pie chart, I listed: 1) Write a book (50%), and 2) Learn to blog (25%) before adding the final category. I felt good about these two.

The pie chart represented how I planned to allocate my time—on a daily basis—over the next three months. Writing was definitely my highest priority at 50%.

I estimated I'd have six productive hours during any given day. In my office job, where I was working a minimum eight hour day, only about six hours were uninterrupted. A lot of my time was consumed by meetings, calls, emails, etc. And I spent a lot of time switching tasks, which ended up consuming time and made me less productive. But during my *layoff reboot*, I had more focused time and significantly fewer interruptions. I was no longer tethered to responding quickly to emails or being called into fire-drill meetings.

As a beginning writer, I was able to write intensely for two hours a day, a number I worked up to slowly. I allocated the rest of my day to other tasks requiring less brainpower such as emails, taking online courses, reading entrepreneurship books, and taking care of small administrative tasks.

And here I have a confession to make. In the very beginning of my time off, I made a project management blunder. I overscheduled myself.

I naively thought that I could take on more goals at one time. I told myself "Hey, I have eight hours to fill up with all these important things I want to do." I tried to add more to my pie chart. I thought I could also fit in time to volunteer and get an additional certification.

I quickly found out that writing and learning alone completely consumed me. I was using my brain in new and complex ways. I was exhausted at times and swept up in the exhilaration of being creative. I had to remember to take breaks!

Don't make the mistake I did of trying to plan something into every minute of your eight hours. This didn't work out for me at all, and I had to ditch the original pie chart I made, which contained a lot more.

A friend of mine, who quit his job around the same time, also experienced this. Like me, at first he thought he would have a lot of time open up without a full-time job. He also had a long list of goals he wanted to tick off. Recently, he shared that he accomplished about 20% of what he had expected. I'm not saying he's wrong for going after many goals instead of a few. You have to find what works best for you.

In month one, I spent nearly all my time focused on writing my book and learning the entrepreneurial side--how to self-publish and market a book. I focused on this, ignoring everything else except a few housekeeping must-do items.

It was an intense time, and I was completely wrapped up in writing, which paid off. I was able to finish writing the first draft of my book in a single month. Before my *layoff reboot* was over, I published. Not bad at all for a beginner!

Focus on your biggest goals one at a time, and be sure to carve a piece of your day for the unexpected. This included my family obligations, household (e.g., shopping/cleaning), and health (e.g., working out and healthy food planning).

Some part of your day will inevitably fall out of your control. In project management, this is the risk. Some things will go your way, but others won't. It's a good idea to factor in buffer time. For example, I was able to pump out my first draft much faster than I expected—but I underestimated the time it would take to edit, publish, and market. And even your best-planned days won't always go perfectly. I left some wiggle room for handling unexpected events. I have a tendency to beat myself up if my plans don't go perfectly, and adding in buffer time gave me flexibility in case something came up, or if I didn't feel well on a given day.

The pie chart ended up being my guide for

structuring my day, and ultimately each month of my time off.

My final (more focused and realistic) pie chart is below:

Now, a final sanity check. Ask yourself again, "Will you be proud of what you accomplish at the end of your *layoff reboot*?"

Daily life would march on. There would be household, family, and social events. But I would have my first book published, and my first blogging website up and running within three months of concentrated effort.

For me, this would be a huge accomplishment and a dream come true. This would give me the confidence I needed for whatever came next. Whether I decided to return to full time employment or try a new career path, I didn't want to wind up doing something I didn't love.

This exercise makes you realize just how much one can do in a short timeframe once you have focused goals. The key to making this happen, though, is discipline.

You can always revisit your secondary goals. In fact, I scheduled a monthly reminder on my calendar to revisit my mind map and pie chart. I wanted to come back to my other goals, but only when the time was right.

By building my pie chart, I was satisfied with the way I would spend my time during my *layoff reboot*. The tool let me organize an entire month of my time, and with everything so clearly mapped out, I could see a path to success. Printing out my pie chart and hanging it above my workspace helped keep me on track.

Keep in mind, this process is about being flexible and self-correcting. I spent nearly the entire first month writing, because it was important I develop a writing habit. I wrote each morning as I woke and grabbed a coffee, and in the afternoons I taught myself about self-publishing by reading books and watching webinars.

It was great, and I learned a lot, but sometimes I needed a break from the intensity of focusing so heavily on writing and publishing. So I fit in a few project management webinars, which helped earn me credits. When I first started out I thought I would be as focused on writing as I was on beefing up my project management skills. This turned out not to be the case at all, and you, too, might find your interests shifting as you continue on your *layoff reboot*. This is to be expected. You're discovering what gets you excited.

I discovered that what I loved most was the process of writing and self-publishing. It was incredibly exciting. Although just as hard work and fast-paced as my corporate job had been, it was far more satisfying to me. I now had a creative outlet, something that had been stifled for years. But it might not have worked out so well for me. If you find during this process that the goal you chose isn't working out, or if it just doesn't feel right, put it on the backburner. Move on to the next unexplored area on your mind map until you find what works for you.

This is especially important in that critical first month or two, as you're adapting to your situation post-layoff. Sometimes what we think may energize us isn't always what will do the trick.

Some things I just find tedious, and that's how you know something drains you. When I start a task and then find excuses to procrastinate, I know it's time to move on, even if I can't explain why.

The most important thing is being able to look back and be satisfied with your accomplishments. Will you look back at the end and appreciate your journey, and how you spent your time?

Create a daily schedule

Once my pie chart was ready, I planned how I would spend my days during my reboot. With this tool I was able to establish, and mostly stick to, a daily routine. I wasn't always perfect—sometimes I was in a "zone" and skipped breaks, or sometimes I tended to other activities such as trip planning. But using a daily schedule kept me, more or less, consistent. Building habits, and having a consistent schedule, meant using my precious time off wisely.

The actual schedule I followed, and kept on my wall, is below. My one BIG goal (book writing)—was half of my day, since it was so important to me. I also had a decent block of time for my second goal—learning to blog. With an open space of time in the late afternoon, I took care of anything miscellaneous that popped up. Sometimes I caught up on reading, or enjoyed time outside.

7:00-8:00 Morning Routine / Journal

8:00-10:00 **(Goal #1)** Write my book

10:00-10:30 Break and emails

10:30-12:00 **(Goal #1 continued)** Work on my book—writing, editing, and learning about self-publishing

12:00-1:00 Lunch / work out

<u>1:00-3:00</u> **(Goal #2)** Learn to blog

<u>3:00-3:30</u> Break and emails

<u>3:30-on</u>: Open for family, social activities, and miscellaneous

<u>10:00</u> bedtime

Of course, unexpected things will happen. You may encounter difficulty in sticking to a daily schedule, especially if you have little ones or other side business ventures going on. Try to avoid over-planning your day. One tip is to allocate larger blocks of time. For example, there were days where I set aside two 3-hour sessions—one in the morning for writing, and one in the afternoon for learning about the technical side of publishing/marketing. In between those times, I checked emails.

Step Three: Develop an Action Plan

With your own pie chart in hand, it's time to develop an action plan. This last step ensures you have the tools you need to plan your goals in more detail. This will ultimately help keep you on track.

I was able to complete the three exercises laid out in this book: 1) Mind mapping, 2) Prioritization, and 3) Action Plan in two weeks. The time you need may differ from my experience. Once done, you'll be on a solid path to exploring long-lost interests, and focusing on what you truly love to do.

Why an action plan?

You've taken the time to lay out your objectives and goals in a mind map. You've ranked and prioritized to establish the things you want to accomplish most. Pause a moment to take this all in. This is an incredible achievement.

You now have a roadmap for accomplishing big things. An action plan is just a way to make sure you'll use your roadmap effectively. A good one will help you lay out your schedule week-by-week, and day-by-day.

Creating your action plan

It's essential to have an organized plan for your day. Think back to the importance of establishing routine and discipline. A well-planned schedule is the key to success, and habits are important for developing discipline. It's essential to make your new goals a part of your daily routine. If you have a goal to write a book in three months, and you end up waiting until midway through month two to get started, you're setting yourself up for disappointment.

Having a self-imposed schedule may be tough to adjust to at first. After all, you don't have to go into an office anymore. Gone are the eight hours a day spent working on someone else's stuff! You get to choose your own path. You get to decide how you want to spend your day. Just remember, it's important to maintain focus. Cherish this opportunity to develop your skills and learn something new, something challenging. Something rewarding.

For me, developing the practice of writing first thing every morning opened my eyes and awakened my creativity. It was something I knew I would enjoy, but I'd always struggled getting started. During my three-month reboot I read several books about writing and self-publishing that were extremely helpful. The authors changed my point of view, and I started to realize that I needed to just take action and start writing.

When you start a new endeavor, whether it's writing or learning to play the tuba, practice is essential. This is nothing new. "I get it" you're saying to yourself. But the problem is most people know this, but don't take action. Learning a new skill or developing your craft is similar to building muscle; it's about putting in time. Every single day. Consistency is everything.

Breaking down the work

Now you've laid out a daily schedule to start working toward your most important goal. This is where you need to spend some time planning how you'll break down the work you need to do to get to a finished product—whether it's your first book, or something else.

A work breakdown structure (WBS) comes from the project management world. It's defined by the Project Management Institute as "the process of subdividing project deliverables and project work into smaller, more manageable components, and it provides a structured vision of what has to be delivered."

This is a fancy way of saying that any project or goal you have needs to be broken down into tasks you must do to finish. It makes the whole project less daunting. If I say I'm going to write for two hours every day that sounds more manageable (and less overwhelming) than saying: "I'm going to write a book."

Your own steps should include any research or learning you may need to do. It may include signing up for a class or a workshop. You may need to plan time simply to brainstorm ideas.

One you've written down the initial steps, think about what other steps you'll need to complete to get to the finish line. Writing a book can be straightforward, since you just need to complete one chapter at a time—after you decide what your book will be about, of course, and how long you want it to be.

Let's consider something else, like starting your own online business. If entrepreneurship is completely new to you, your first steps will include lots of research and learning. Your tasks would break down into something like this:

BIG GOAL: Start Your Online Business

I. LEARNING

(a) Read top five books about internet entrepreneurship.

(b) Research popular blogs and start reading posts.

(c) Come up with 10 potential business ideas daily (no matter how wacky or far-fetched).

(d) Narrow down your ideas to the top five.

II. PLANNING

(a) Identify 2-3 entrepreneurs who are doing something similar to your ideas.

(b) Subscribe to their blogs/websites if applicable and reach out to them to see if they will discuss their lessons learned in starting their business.

(c) Finalize your business idea(s) that you want to go after.

(d) Create your business plan.

(e) Seek input from others in your network who have started online businesses.

III. EXECUTING

(a) Gather necessary materials to start your business.

(b) Start designing/producing your product or creating content for your services.

(c) Start selling your product / service.

And so on.

This should give you a good idea of how you can start to break down your goals into the more manageable actions. The important thing at first is just to get the tasks down on paper. Don't worry about not capturing everything the first time. Just get it down.

You'll undoubtedly make tweaks to your work breakdown structure along the way. This will happen as you start to learn more about your new craft, or the industry you're trying to shift to. Think of it as a living document. You'll want to track progress on a weekly basis to make sure you're not getting stuck somewhere.

You don't need to record every detail, of course, but you *will* want to identify the "chunks" of work. Even before I started writing my book I knew I needed to 1) hire an editor, and 2) allocate time for an editor to review and send back. There will be iterations back and forth. Rather than obsessing over the details and getting all the steps into the action plan, I simply record that it's a three-step process.

Step 1: Hire editor (3-4 days).

Step 2: Editorial review (1 week).

Step 3: Finalize editorial feedback (1 week plus half a week just in case).

Using this method, and after adding in buffer time, I know I needed about three weeks to get my book edited. This helped me plan out my time, and gave me an easy way to figure out if my book was getting stuck somewhere in the editing process.

Summary

After following the steps in this chapter, you'll have a finished action plan which consists of:

1. Your most important goals clearly laid out in a **simple pie chart**.

2. A **daily schedule** that can guide how you spend your day. Best to keep this posted in a visible place.

3. A **work break down structure** that lays out the tasks that you'll need to accomplish your goals.

8 TIPS FOR SUCCESS

As my *layoff reboot* went on, I learned a lot about how I worked without a boss. It was an adjustment from the years spent at my 9-to-5 job, but I learned what worked for me. Here are some tips I found helpful.

Set a designated time for emails

Ideally, I only process emails three to four times per day. In my former work life, I spent countless hours working on emails. Between emails and meetings, it's a wonder I got anything useful done.

I don't want to go back to that life. Email processing can feel productive in the moment, but ultimately I'm not being creative. I recommend, as do many productivity books out there, to "batch" your email processing to only a few times each day. Perhaps once mid-morning, once in the afternoon, and once in the evening.

If I decide to make a career switch, I'll inevitably be getting more emails. At that point, I'll reassess how much time I need to spend on them, and whether I can automate responses or delegate to someone.

Limit distractions

Are you someone who spends a lot of time checking and keeping up with social media? I can zone out on Facebook for hours at a time without realizing, so I try to limit the time I spend checking social media to when I have down time. I use my phone to check when I'm waiting in line, or riding public transportation. I'll treat myself when I take short breaks after I've accomplished other tasks.

Television goes in the distraction category as well. Binge watching a series should be saved for designated times. With so much new content out there, focus on quality, not quantity, of series. I have a few series I follow closely. Often I wait until four or five people recommend a show as "must see" before I'll start a new show.

Journaling

One of the most powerful habits I picked up after getting laid off was journaling. I put my laptop at my kitchen table and each morning, as I'm sipping my coffee, I write for 5-10 minutes.

You can write about anything you like. I focus on positive thoughts, setting the tone for the rest of my day. I write about what I'm grateful for, and about the goals I want to accomplish that day.

Writing first thing in the morning works best for me. You can choose to journal when convenient. Some people choose to write at night and dissect their day after it's happened.

Avoid analysis paralysis

When you're deciding what to pursue, you'll need to read books on your topic and spend time researching. But be careful about getting hung up in preliminary steps. You don't need to read 10-20 books before you get started, and research can become a procrastination tool. I recommend choosing just two or three books. In my case, I knew I wanted to self-publish an e-book, but had no idea where to start.

I read Chandler Bolt's _Book Launch_, which gave me everything I needed to get started. After that, I followed his advice and just started writing every single day. I read two more books about self-publishing to gain extra confidence in what I was getting myself into.

Be kind to yourself

There are going to be good and bad days. Don't beat yourself up when you have a bad day. This is a massive change in your life.

As I journeyed down my *layoff reboot*, 80% of my needs for energy and stamina were taken care of by my best attempts at developing healthy habits for diet, exercise and sleep.

I can't say enough about the importance of addressing and making positive changes in these lifestyle areas. In your newly creative life, your brain needs more energy than you used in your work life, when you were just going through the motions and taking orders.

If you're struggling in any areas—diet, exercise, sleep, I recommend you seek help. See your doctor, hire a nutritionist, a trainer or enroll in an online program. There are plenty of free and low-cost online classes, books and tutorials as well.

Information diet

Tim Ferris talks about going on a low-information diet in his book, *Four-Hour Work Week*. Think of the flood of information we face every day. How can you trim that down?

First off, spend time unsubscribing to unwanted emails and newsletters. A mental trick I used was thinking about going on a long trip abroad. Knowing that I'd want to maximize my time in a new locale, would I still need a newsletter about concerts that I never attend anyway?

If an invitation comes your way or people ask you to join a group—consider whether it fits with your goals. If it's not a goal on your mind map, don't accept. It's hard to say no sometimes, but your focus needs to stay on you.

An exception to this rule, however, is for stress relief. After all, we're not robots, and although you're absorbed with exploring a new direction, you don't want to lose yourself. Keep doing those things you find rewarding that are completely different from the new world you're living in now.

I made sure to keep up with social plans and found ways to get out of the house. I signed up for a 5K race and still managed to take two separate trips out of state. These things were important to keep me grounded.

Dare to take risks

I'm hoping your layoff will change your outlook on life the way it did mine. I had always dreamed of writing a book, but I never thought my dream was realistic. It was a "someday" goal. But my layoff forced me to re-evaluate my life's direction, and today I've achieved my dream.

The best part of all this was that it opened my eyes to how much I disliked what I was doing before. I'd been at the same company so long I'd gotten comfortable. But I lacked the creativity outlet I needed. I went through the last few years dreading

Mondays and living for the weekends.

Dare to pursue that "someday" thing that you've been putting off, and I promise, you'll be much happier.

Accountability partner

Many people benefit from being held accountable to another person or to a group. If you can't find someone who's in a similar situation, find someone who has certain goals to meet. You can meet with, Skype, or FaceTime with them on a regular basis, and give one another updates on how you're progressing toward your goals.

This works best when you each have specific weekly goals you're trying to accomplish, and you both establish deadlines for reporting your progress. I found an accountability partner who's pursuing a lifestyle change after quitting her job voluntarily. Soon we'll meet to share our experiences.

In addition, being accountable to someone can be a powerful tool to avoid procrastination. It's never fun to meet up only to have to say you didn't complete your tasks for that week.

9 PUT YOUR REBOOT PLAN INTO ACTION

My hope at this point is you've succeeded in coming up with your action plan, and are ready to get going.

Be sure to keep your mind map *visible*. Post it above your desk, or at least review it every day (e.g. at the start of your morning routine), and journal about how you got closer to completing your goals.

For myself, establishing a theme for each month was also helpful. My theme for the first month was starting a morning routine and writing daily. Month two was all about finishing and publishing my e-book. Month three was writing blog content every day, and volunteering. Keep to no more than one or two themes per month. Otherwise you run the risk of becoming overwhelmed.

Set up monthly check-ins

Here are some final instructions before you head off on your own journey. Set up some checkpoints with yourself in your calendar. Once per month worked for me. These will be times where you'll do a "lessons learned" appointment with yourself.

Ask yourself the following:

1. What did I accomplish this month?

2. Am I proud of what I accomplished?

3. What can I do better next time?

4. What are my goals for next month? Will I be proud of them and are they realistic?

These checkpoint reviews will be eye-opening. They'll help you realize if there's something preventing you from meeting your goals each month and help steer you back on track if you've gotten distracted or off-base.

IN CLOSING

Thank you for reading my book and listening to my story! Sharing my *layoff reboot* journey is a dream come true. I hope you take something away from my experience, and find at least one tool helpful for your own employment situation. And I hope you learn more about yourself, and are able to make a change if you're not doing what you love.

Even if you're employed but something just doesn't feel right, my hope is that you can apply the tools in this book on a smaller scale. Take a few minutes each day to "immerse" yourself in an area that piques your interest. It might be as simple as picking up a few books on a topic you enjoy. That's how I started learning about writing and self-publishing. Let it be the start of something new. It just might change how you look at your career—and your life.

I would love to hear your story, or if you have any questions as you start your own *layoff reboot*. Please drop me an email at info@projectmanagerwriter.com or find out more at projectmanagerwriter.com. There you'll find the free downloadable companion workbook.

You can find my Facebook page at www.facebook.com/courtkennwrite. Join other readers and learn more about my writing and upcoming book projects.

Reviews on Amazon help other readers find books. I would be grateful if you would leave a helpful and honest review of this book on Amazon.

I wish you success in rebooting and discovering what you love to do!

Thank you.

Courtney Kenney

ABOUT THE AUTHOR

Courtney Kenney is an author and book launch consultant. She spent sixteen years working as a Project Manager at technology companies. She left corporate life behind to become a freelance Project Manager and runs her own business helping entrepreneurs launch bestselling books and grow their author platforms.

She lives in Chicago with her husband and loves walking, exploring new neighborhoods, traveling, and playing in a competitive skeeball league.

Visit her website, projectmanagerwriter.com, where she writes about becoming a more productive and prosperous author. Get a Free eBook: ***Productive Author Roadmap: Write More, Streamline Your Publishing, Simplify Your Marketing, and Adopt a Productive Author Mindset.***

Connect with Courtney online:
Projectmanagerwriter.com/contact
Twitter.com/pmpwriter
Facebook.com/courtkennwrite
Instagram/authorunleashed

More books by Courtney Kenney:
Unleash Your Author: Write a Book in 30 Days